JOHN THOMPSON'S
EASIEST PIANO COL

CW00460137

FIRST FILM MUSIC

This collection of popular film songs is intended as supplementary material for those working through **John Thompson's Easiest Piano Course** Parts 2–4. The pieces may also be used for sight reading practice by more advanced students.

Dynamics and phrasing have been deliberately omitted from the earlier pieces, since they are not introduced until Part 3 of the Easiest Piano Course, and initially the student's attention should be focused on playing notes and rhythms accurately. Outline fingering has been included, and in general the hand is assumed to remain in a five-finger position until a new fingering indicates a position shift. The fingering should suit most hands, although logical alternatives are always possible.

Billy Elliot Scene from 'Swan Lake'

Music by Pyotr Ilyich Tchaikovsky

Gracefully

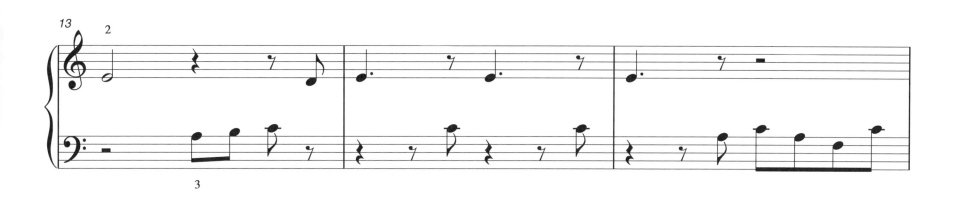

Fantasia The Sorcerer's Apprentice

Music by Paul Dukas

Swiftly, with energy

Willy Wonka & The Chocolate Factory Pure Imagination

Words & Music by Leslie Bricusse & Anthony Newley

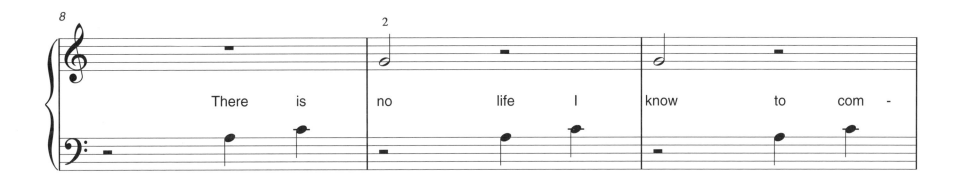

There is no life I know to com -

- pare with pure i - ma - gi - na - tion. Liv - ing there, you'll be

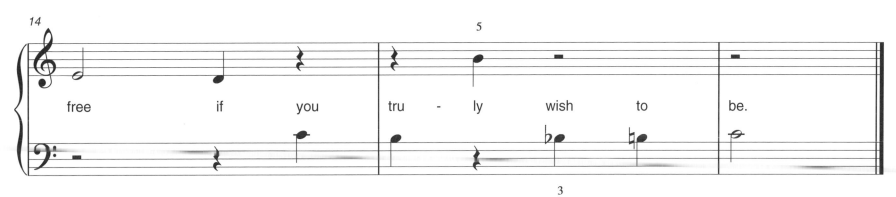

free if you tru - ly wish to be.

Ratatouille Theme

Music by Michael Giacchino

With feeling

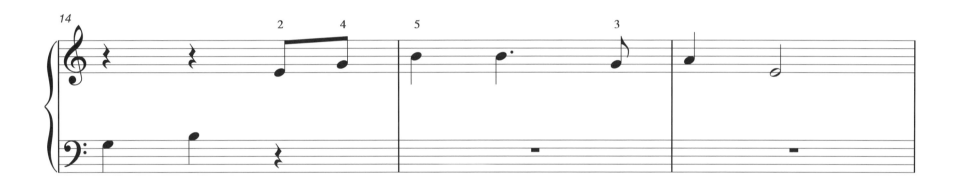

Chitty Chitty Bang Bang Hushabye Mountain

Words & Music by Richard Sherman & Robert Sherman

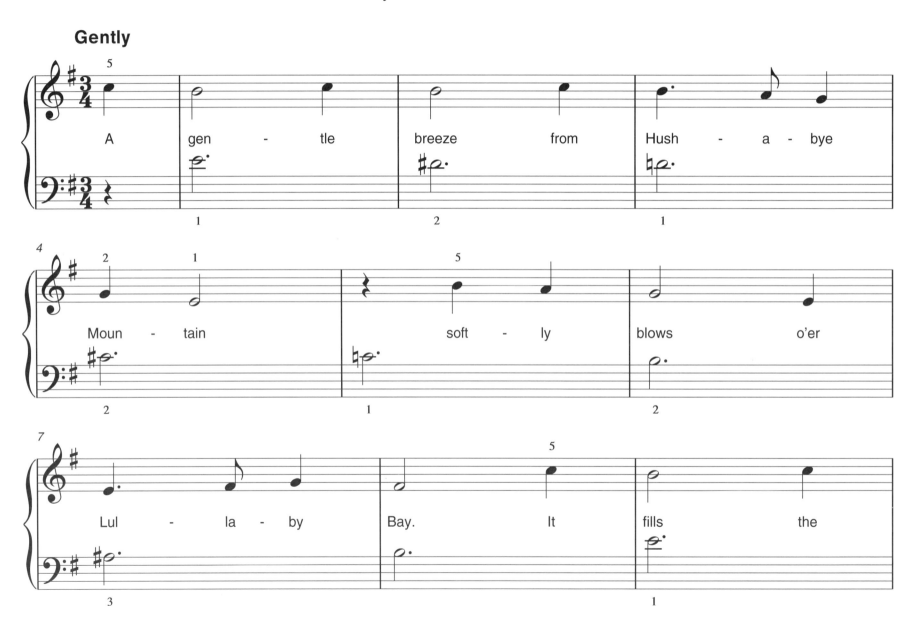

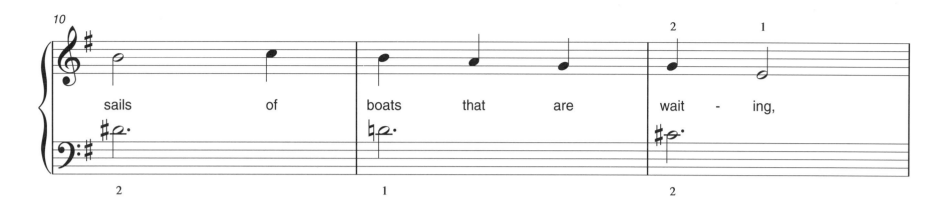

sails   of   boats   that   are   wait -   ing,

wait - ing   to   sail   your   wor - ries a -   way.

Spirited Away Reprise

Music by Joe Hisaishi

Babe 'Organ' Symphony

Music by Camille Saint-Saëns

Stately

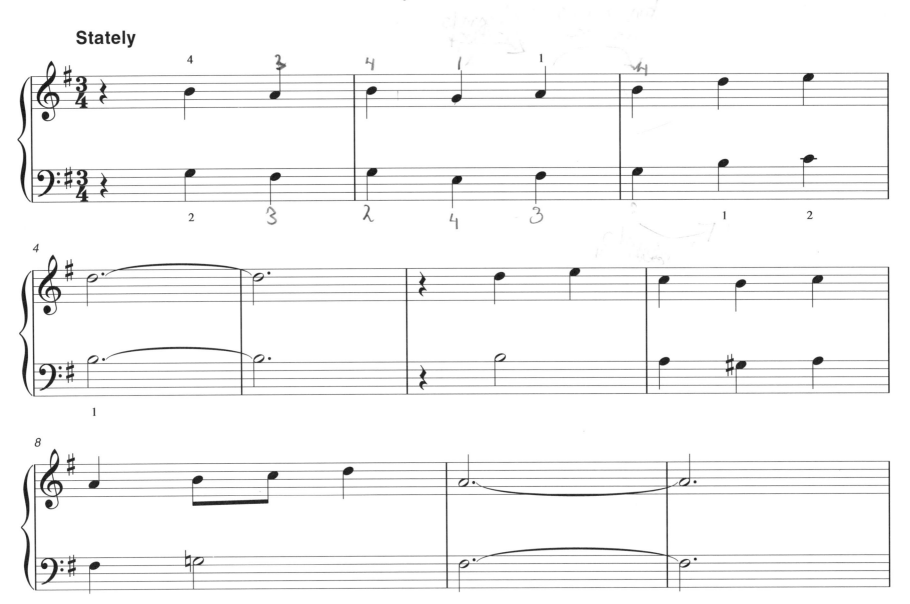

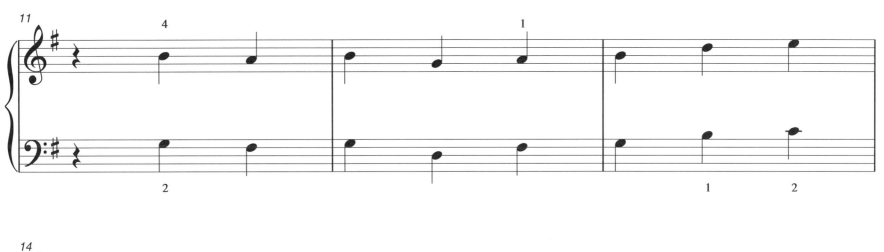

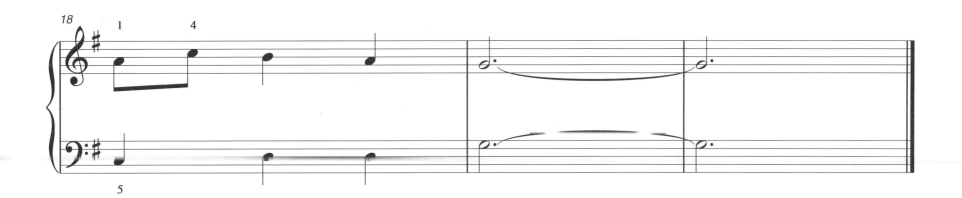

The Lion King Circle Of Life

Music by Elton John
Words by Tim Rice

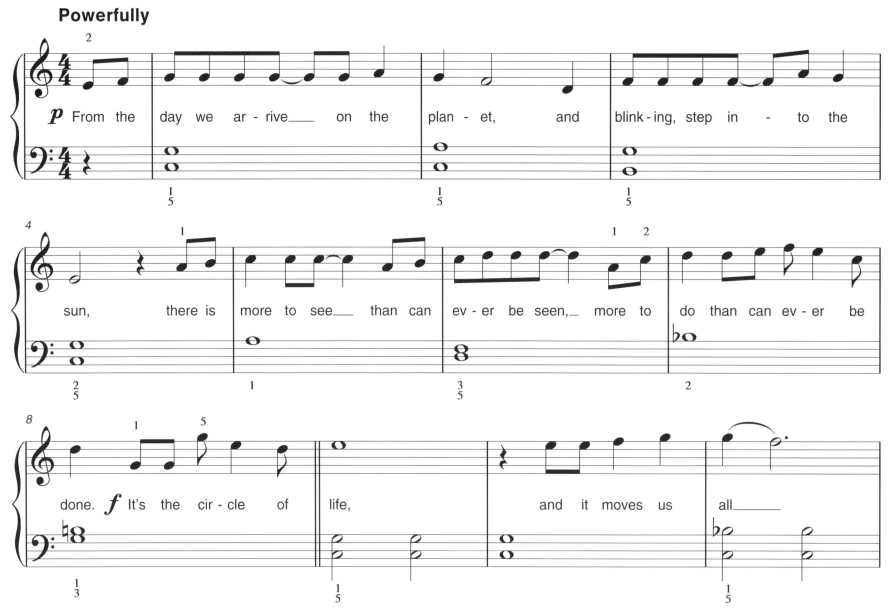

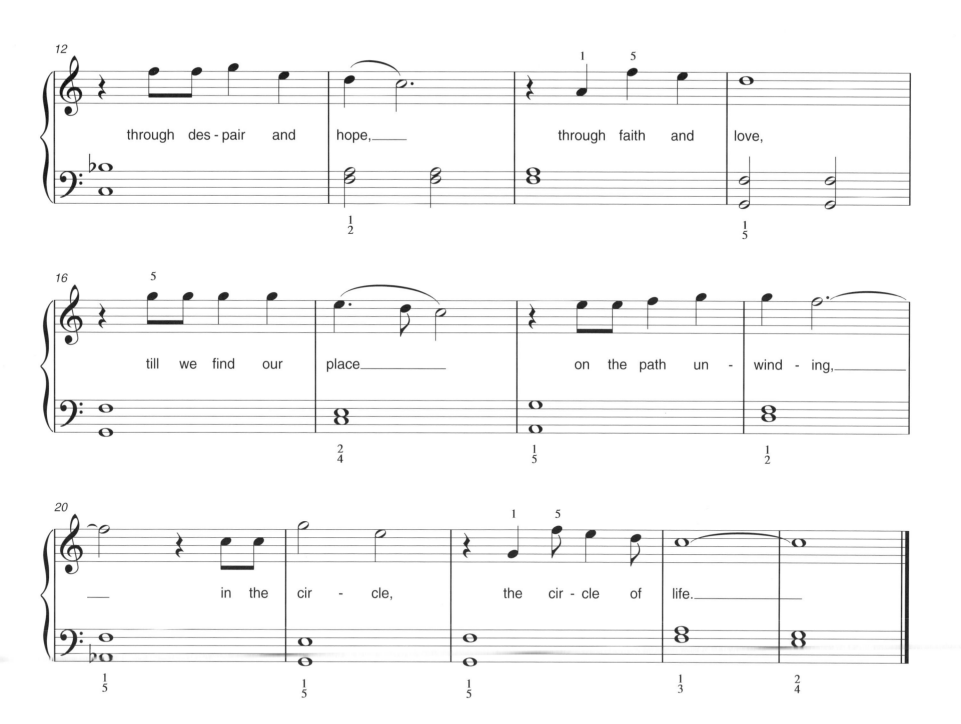

Wallace And Gromit Theme

Music by Julian Nott

Fantasia 2000 Finale from 'The Carnival Of The Animals'

Music by Camille Saint-Saëns

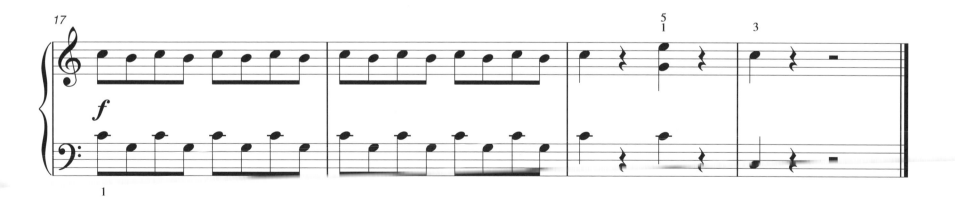

Finding Nemo Beyond The Sea

Music by Charles Trenet & Albert Lasry
Original French Lyrics by Charles Trenet, English Lyrics by Jack Lawrence

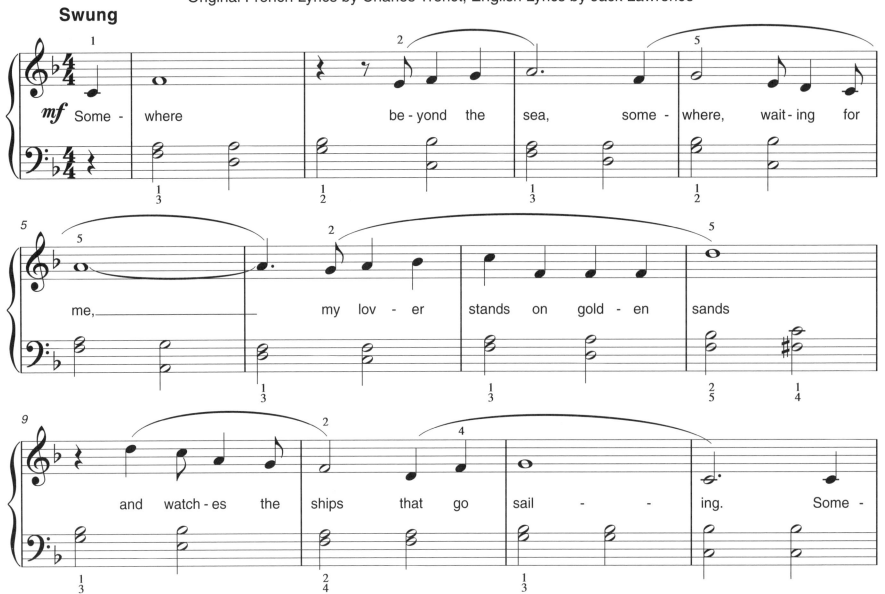

Monsters, Inc. If I Didn't Have You

Words & Music by Randy Newman

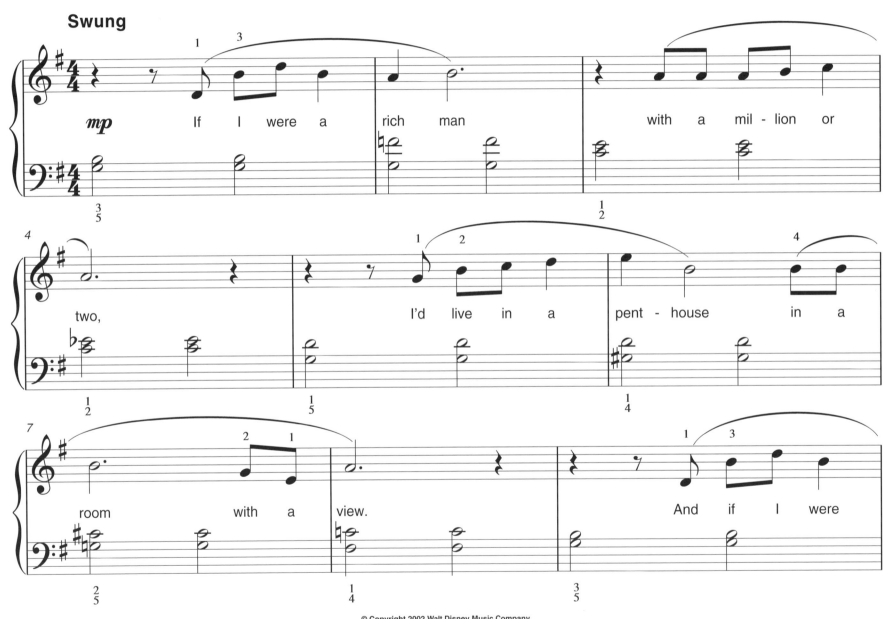

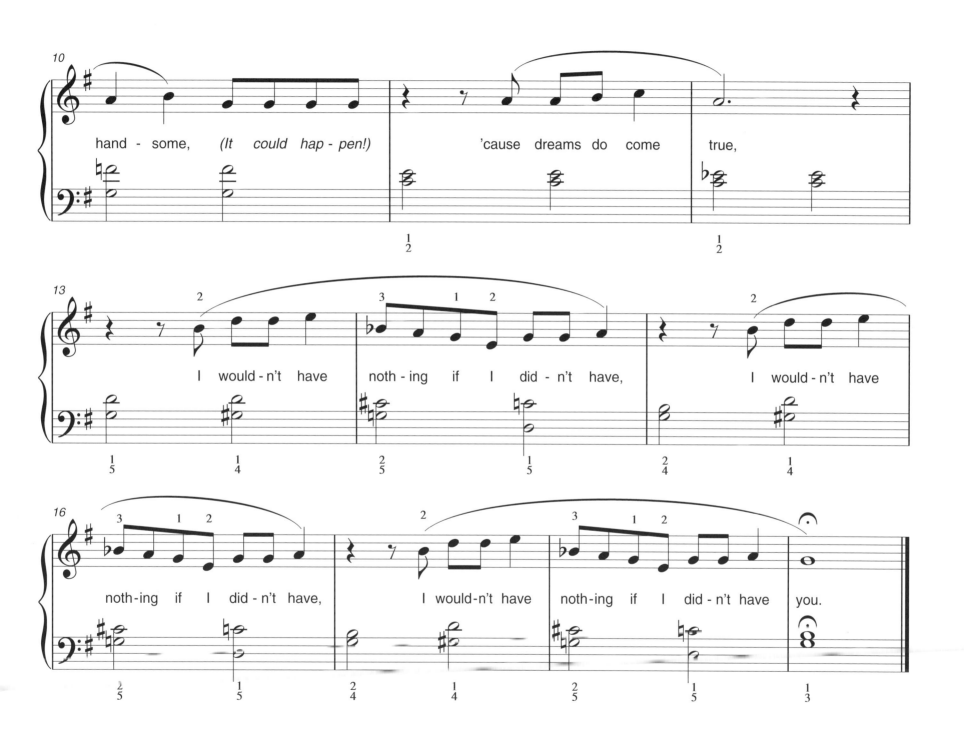

Toy Story 2 When She Loved Me

Words & Music by Randy Newman

Through the sum-mer and the fall we had each oth-er, that was all; just she and I to-geth-er, like it was meant to be. And when she was lone-ly, I was there to com-fort her, and I knew that she loved me.

rall.

Shrek I'm A Believer

Words & Music by Neil Diamond

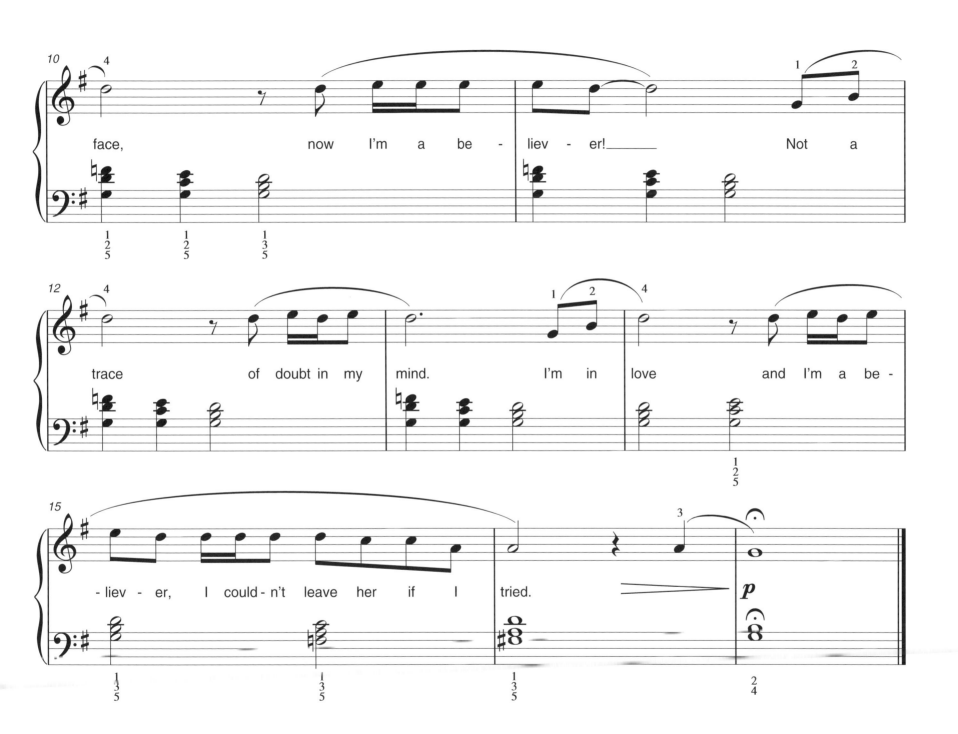

The Simpsons Theme

Music by Danny Elfman

© Copyright 2014 The Willis Music Company
Florence, Kentucky, USA. All Rights Reserved.

Exclusive Distributors:
Music Sales Limited
Newmarket Road, Bury St Edmunds, Suffolk IP33 3YB, UK.
Music Sales Pty Limited
Units 3-4, 17 Willfox Street, Condell Park, NSW 2200, Australia.

Order No. WMR101354
ISBN: 978-1-78305-471-8

Arranged by Christopher Hussey.
Arrangements and engravings supplied by Camden Music Services.
Edited by Sam Lung.

Printed in the EU.